Python Fastlane
Crash Course

The Smart Way To Learn Python Proramming

Copyright © 2020 Martin Goldmeyr

All rights reserved.

Imprint: Independently published
ISBN: 9798633014228

Introduction

Computer Programming is one of the most important skills for engineers and scientists in the 21st century. Python is the number one programming language in various fields. Did you ever want to learn to program? Python is a beginner-friendly and easy-to-learn programming language, even if you have never written a line of code before.

With Python you can code console and desktop applications, but also web-based applications and even programs for the very famous single-board computer: The Raspberry Pi.

Python is also the most important programming language for scientists all over the world, and the most famous artificial intelligence software is written in Python.

But although Python is so powerful, it is easy to learn. This book guides you through a journey to learn the most famous programming language in the world. With step-by-step instructions and explanations of all important core features, you will soon write your own computer programs and explore the world of software development.

Table of Contents

Introduction 4
About This Book.. 10
Chapter 1- Getting Started with Python 12
    What is Python?... 12
    Installing Python 13
    Script vs. Interactive Programming Modes.......................... 13
    First Python Program 14
    Indentation 16
    Quotation 17
    Python Comments 17
Chapter 2- Variables and Data Types 20
    Multiple Assignment 22
    Python Numbers 23
    Python Strings 26
    Python Lists 28
    Python Tuples 29
    Lists vs. Tuples.. 31
    Python Dictionaries... 39
    Datatype Conversion... 40
Chapter 3- Python Operators 43
    Arithmetic Operators 43
    Comparison Operators.. 45
Chapter 4- Flow Control 48
    The "if" statement 48

The "if...elif...else" statement 51

The "elif" Statement 53

The Nested "if" 55

Chapter 5- Loops and Control Statements 58

For Loop 58

"RANGE()" function 58

While Loop 63

Loop Control 66

break Statement 66

continue Statement 68

pass Statement 70

Chapter 6- Functions 72

Defining Functions 72

Function Parameters 74

Function Parameter Defaults 78

An Anonymous Function 80

The "return" Statement 81

The Variable Scope 82

Chapter 7- Error and Exception Handling 86

Raising Exceptions 90

Exception Objects 91

Custom Exception Class 93

Chapter 8- Working with Files 96

Opening and Closing Files 96

Reading from Files 101

File Positions 102

Renaming Files 103

Deleting Files 105

Creating Directories 105

Changing Directory 106

Current Working Directory 107

Deleting Directories 108

Chapter 9- Python Classes and Objects 109

Instantiating Classes 111

Accessing Attributes 112

Built-in Attributes for Classes 114

Destroying Objects in Python (Garbage Collection) 116

Method Overriding in Python 119

Data Hiding 120

Inheritance 122

Operator Overloading 126

Conclusion 128

About This Book

Python is one of the most famous programming languages today. With python, one can accomplish a wide range of tasks. One can use Python to write programs to perform both basic and complex tasks. Python can be used for the development of desktop applications, website applications, game applications, and even distributed applications. The good thing with Python is that it is a simple programming language, and anyone can get started with it. It is the best language for anyone who needs to begin computer programming. The process of getting started with Python is also easy as you only need a basic text editor like Notepad on Windows and the Python interpreter, which is easy to install. When you get these installed on your computer, you can begin to write and run your Python programs. For Linux users, this is easy as the latest Linux versions come installed with the Python interpreter. What you may have to do is only to update it to the latest version. The installation of Python on other operating systems is easy as you only need to download the Python setup file from the official python's website and begin the installation process. During the installation process, one is provided with simple on-screen instructions making the process easy to follow through. This book is a guide for any person who wants to get started with Python programming.

The author takes you through various steps to help you transition from a complete Python beginner to a Python expert. Enjoy reading!

Chapter 1- Getting Started with Python

What is Python?

Python is a powerful and multipurpose programming language. It was developed by Guido van Rossum. Python is well-known for its easy syntax, and this makes it the best language for anyone who is a complete beginner to computer programming. Programmers have found it easier to write and read programs written in Python that those written in other programming languages like C, C++, Java, etc.

You are allowed to use and distribute Python for free. It is free and open-source. You are also allowed to make changes to the Python source code so as to meet your needs. Python is made up of a large community of developers who make constant changes to it.

With Python, you can write a program with greater functionality using only a few lines of code. This will amaze you once we start writing our Python codes. Python is also an object-oriented programming language. This means that it supports the features and concepts of object-oriented programming, such as the use of classes, objects, etc. it is interpreted, meaning that it has an interpreter instead of a compiler.

Installing Python

You can install and use Python on various operating systems, including Windows, Mac OS X, and the various Linux distributions. The good news is that the newer versions of Linux come with Python installed, so you only have to update it if it is outdated.

To install Python on Windows or Mac OS X, just open the official Python website which you can find by typing the following URL:

python.org

Click the Downloads button and choose the type of operating system that you are using. You will then be able to download the setup file with everything that you need to get started with Python. Once the download is complete, double click the setup file to start the installation process. You will be taken through onscreen instructions, and the Python will be installed on your computer.

Script vs. Interactive Programming Modes

These are the two modes that we can use to write and run our Python scripts. In the script mode of programming, we use a text editor such as Notepad or the Python IDLE to create a file in which we will write and save our Python code. The name of the file should be written with a .py extension to signify that it is a Python file. The code is then executed from that file at a go. One of the ways of doing this is opening the command prompt of the operating system and invoking the Python interpreter on the file by typing the following command:

```
python filename
```

The above command should then return the results of the code on the terminal of the operating system.

In the interactive mode of programming, we write the Python code line by line, and the interpreter returns the results immediately. This involves opening the command prompt of the operating system and typing the command *python* on it. This should take you to the Python interactive terminal. This is shown below:

```
C:\Windows\system32>python
Python 3.5.0 (v3.5.0:374f501f4567, Sep 13 2015, 02:27:37) [MSC v.1900 64 bit (AM
D64)] on win32
Type "help", "copyright", "credits" or "license" for more information.
>>>
```

The >>> shows that I am on the Python interactive prompt.

First Python Program

We need to write the first program in Python. Just open the command prompt of your operating system, type the *python* command, and hit the enter key on your keyboard. You will be taken to the Python interactive prompt. Type the following on it and hit the enter key:

```
print("Hello world!")
```

This should work as shown below:

```
C:\Users\admin>python
Python 3.5.0 (v3.5.0:374f501f4567, Sep 13 2015, 02:27:37) [MSC v.1900 64 bit (AMD64)] on win32
Type "help", "copyright", "credits" or "license" for more information.
>>> print("Hello world!")
Hello world!
>>>
```

The code has returned the string *Hello world!*. We have simply invoked the *print()* function, which displays contents. We can also create the above script in a Python file and execute it from there. Just open a text editor like Notepad and create a file named *hello.py*. Add the following line of code to the file then save it:

```
print("Hello world!")
```

Now open the terminal of the operating system and navigate to the directory where you saved the *hello.py* file. In my case, I saved it in local disk F. You can then type the following command on the terminal and hit the enter key on your keyboard:

```
python hello.py
```

This is demonstrated below:

```
C:\Users\admin>F:

F:\>python hello.py
Hello world!

F:\>
```

The code worked successfully!

Indentation

In Python, we don't use braces to group sections of code and as a way of controlling the way the code flows. This is what happens in most programming languages. Instead of this, Python allows us to use line indentation for this.

The number of spaces that should be added to an indentation always varies. However, all statements that belong to the same block should be indented equally. Here is an example:

```
if True:
   print("It is True")
else:
   print("It is False")
```

See the following code that will return an error due to lack of indentation:

```
if True:
print("The answer is:")
print("True")
```

```
else:
    print("The answer is:")
    print("False")
```

This means that in Python, all statements that appear continuously and indented with the same number of spaces will form a block.

Quotation

In Python, we use quotations as a way of denoting string literals. Python allows single, double, and triple quotes for this. The kind of quote you use to start the string should be used to end the quote. You can also use quotes as a way of stretching a string across many lines. The following are valid examples of this:

```
name = 'Nicholas'
sentence = "A short sentence."
paragraph = """A simple paragraph. It is
spanning more than one lines and sentences."""
```

Python Comments

If you use the hash sign (#) outside a string literal, you will be creating a comment. All the strings or words that come after the # to the end of that line will form a comment. Note that the Python interpreter skips comments instead of interpreting them. Here is an example:

```
# A comment
print("Hello world!") # A second comment
```

The comments will not affect or change the output from the string.

In the second line of the above example, it shows that it is possible for you to add a comment on the same line as a statement. However, the comment should come after the statement.

You can comment multiple lines appearing continuously as shown below:

```
# A comment
# Another comment
# Another comment
# Another comment
```

To create multiline comments in Python, which are comments that span multiple lines, we can use double quotes as shown below:

```
'''
A multiline
comment in Python.
'''
```

Chapter 2- Variables and Data Types

The work of variables is to reserve memory locations for us to store data. This means that once a variable is created, some space is reserved in the memory. The variable's value can change over time (that's why it's called a *variable*).

With variables, python programs are made to be more dynamic. In fact, one is able to reference the value of the variable without having to keep on typing it. They can also change its value if there is a need to do so.

A variable can be assigned any name, but this name should not conflict with the name of any function, and the name should not start with a number. This means that you should be careful when giving names to classes, functions, and variables in Python so that their names don't conflict. For example, you know that Python has an inbuilt function named *print*. What will happen if you create a variable with the name *print*? This will lead to a conflict, and the program will result in an error.

In python, a variable is created when it is assigned a value. This also tells the Python interpreter the amount of memory that it should allocate to that variable and the kind of data that can be stored on the memory space reserved for the variable.

The following example demonstrates how to use variables in Python:

```
# Integer variable and value
age = 32

# Floating point variable and value
height   = 16.1

# String variables and values
first_name = "John"
second_name   = "Joel"

print (age)
print (height)
print (first_name)
print (second_name)
```

On execution, the code should return the following:

```
32
16.1
John
Joel
```

We defined 4 variables. The first variable is named *age*, and it should store an integer value. The second variable is named *height*, and it should store a floating-point value. The last two variables should store strings.

To see the value of each variable, we have just typed the name of the variable in the *print* function.

Multiple Assignment

This is the process of assigning a single value to more than one variable. This is supported in Python. Here is an example:

```
x = y = z = 5
```

In the above example, we have three variables, namely x, y, z. All of them have been assigned a single value of 5. You are also allowed to assign many objects to many variables. For example:

```
x, y, z = 4, 8, "John"
```

In the above example, the two integer values will be assigned to variables x and y, respectively, while the string value will be assigned to variable z.

Now that you have known how to define variables and assign values to variables let us discuss the various data types supported in Python.

Python supports different data types. Each variable should belong to one of the data types supported in Python. The data type determines the value that can be assigned to a variable, the type of operation that may be applied to the variable as well as the amount of space assigned to the variable. Let us discuss different data types supported in Python:

Python Numbers

These data types help in storing numeric values. The creation of number objects in Python is done after we have assigned a value to them. Consider the example given below:

```
total = 53
age= 32
```

You are familiar with this as we had discussed it earlier. Also, it is possible for you to delete a reference to a particular number variable. This can be done by using the del statement. This statement takes the following syntax:

```
del variable1[,variable2[,variable3[....,variableN]]]
```

The statement can be used for the deletion of single or multiple variables. This is shown below:

```
del total
del total, age
```

In the first statement, we are deleting a single variable, while in the second statement, we are deleting two variables. If the variables to be deleted are more than two, separate them by use of a comma, and they will be deleted.

In Python, there are four numerical values which are supported:
- int
- float
- complex

In Python3, all integers are represented in the form of long integers.

The Python integer literals belong to the *int* class. Example:
Run the following statements consecutively on the Python interactive interpreter:

```
p=20
p
```

The float is used for storing numeric values with a decimal point. Example:

```
p=20.365
p
```

You can run it on the Python interactive interpreter, and you will observe the following:

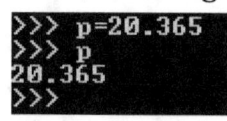

If you are performing an operation with one of the operands being a float and the other being an integer, the result will be a float. Example:

```
5 * 1.5
```

As shown above, the result of the operation is 7.5, which is a float.

Complex numbers are made of real and imaginary parts, with the imaginary part being denoted using a *j*. They can be defined as follows:

```
p = 3 + 7j
```

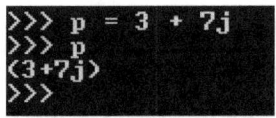

In the above example, 3 is the real part, while 7 is the imaginary part.

Using the function *type()*, we can find out the type of a variable. You only have to pass the name of the variable inside that function as the argument, and its type will be printed. Example:

```
p=10
type(p)
```

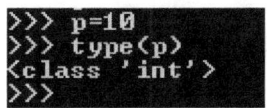

The variable p is of int class, as shown above. You can try it for other variable types, as shown below:

name='john'
type(name)

```
>>> name='john'
>>> type(name)
<class 'str'>
>>>
```

The variable is of the string class, as shown above.

Python Strings

Python strings are a series of characters enclosed within quotes. Use any type of quotes to enclose Python strings, that is, either single, double, or triple quotes. To access string elements, we use the slice operator. String characters begin at index 0, meaning that the first character string is at index 0. This is good when you need to access string characters. To concatenate strings in Python, we use + operator, the asterisk 9*) is used for repetition. Example:

```
#!/usr/bin/python3

welcome = 'Welcome to Python'

# to print the complete string
print (welcome)

# to print the first character of string
print (welcome [0])
```

```
# to print the 3rd to the 7th character of
string
print (welcome [2:7])

# to print from the 5th character of string
print (welcome [4:])

# to print the string two times
print (welcome * 2)

# to print a concatenated string
print (welcome + "\tAgain!")
```

The program prints the following once executed:

```
Welcome to Python
W
lcome
ome to Python
Welcome to PythonWelcome to Python
Welcome to Python        Again!
```

Notice that we have text beginning with # symbol. The symbol denotes the beginning of a comment. The Python print will not act on the text from the symbol to the end of the line. Comments are meant to enhance the readability of code by giving an explanation. We defined a string named *welcome* with the value *Welcome to Python*. The *print (welcome[0])* statement helps us access the first character of the string. Hence it prints *T*. You also notice that the space between the two words is counted as a character.

Python Lists

Lists consist of items enclosed within square brackets ([]), and the items are separated using commas (,). They are similar to the C arrays. Although all array elements must belong to a similar type, lists support the storage of items belonging to different types in a single list.

We use the slice operator ([ ] and [:]) for accessing the elements of a list. The indices start at 0 and end at -1. Also, the plus symbol (+) represents the concatenation operator, while the asterisk (*) represents the repetition operator. Example:

```
#!/usr/bin/python3

listA = [ 'joel', 3400 , 7.70, 'sister', 23.11 ]
listB = [100, 'sister']

# will print the complete list
print (listA)

# will print the first element of the list
print (listA[0])

# will print the elements starting from  the 2nd till 3rd
print (listA[1:3])

# will print the elements starting from the 3rd element
```

```
print (listA[2:])

# will print the list two times
print (listB * 2)

# will print a concatenated lists
print (listA + listB)
```

There is no much difference in what is happening in the above code compared to the previous one for strings. When executed, the program outputs:

```
['joel', 3400, 7.7, 'sister', 23.11]
joel
[3400, 7.7]
[7.7, 'sister', 23.11]
[100, 'sister', 100, 'sister']
['joel', 3400, 7.7, 'sister', 23.11, 100, 'sister']
```

In the statement "print (listA)", we print the contents of listA. Note that each element is treated to be at its own index as a whole, for example, element 'joel' is treated as a single element of a list at index 0.

Python Tuples

Python tuples are similar to lists with the difference being after creating a tuple, you cannot add, delete or change the tuple elements. Tuple elements should be enclosed within parenthesis (). Example:

```
#!/usr/bin/python3

# creating an empty tuple, that is, no data
tp1 = ()
```

```
tp2 = (22,34,55)

# creating a tuple from an array
tp3 = tuple([10,23,78,110,89])

# creating tuple from a string
tp4 = tuple("xyz")

print (tp1)
print (tp2)
print (tp3)
print (tp4)
```

The values of the 4 tuples will be printed:

```
()
(22, 34, 55)
(10, 23, 78, 110, 89)
('x', 'y', 'z')
```

There are a number of functions that can be applied on tuples. Example:

```
#!/usr/bin/python3
tp1 = (21, 13, 32, 20, 76)

print("The minimum element in the tuple is", min(tp1))

print("The sum of tuple elements is", sum(tp1))

print("The maximum element in the tuple is", max(tp1))

print("The tuple has a length of", len(tp1))
```

When executed, it gives this result:

```
The minimum element in the tuple is 13
The sum of tuple elements is 162
The maximum element in the tuple is 76
The tuple has a length of 5
```

First, we called the *min()* function which returns the smallest element in the tuple. We then called the *sum()* function which returned the total sum of tuple elements. The *max()* function returned the maximum element in the tuple. The *len()* function counted all elements in the tuple and returned their number.

You can use the slice operator to access some of the tuple elements, not all. Example:

```
#!/usr/bin/python3
tp = (21, 27, 46, 58, 68)
print(tp[0:2])
```

When executed, it prints:

```
(21, 27)
```

We have used the slice operator to access elements from index 0 to index 2 in the tuple. Note that tuple elements begin at index 0.

Lists vs. Tuples

A sequence forms the basic data structure in Python. Every element in a Python list is assigned a number marking its position, and this number is referred to as the *index*. The indexes begin at 0, meaning that the first sequence element is at index 0 while the last element is at index *n-1*, where *n* is the total number of elements in the sequence.

Python comes with six types of built-in types, with lists and tuples forming the most popular ones. Let us discuss these:

Lists consist of items enclosed within square brackets ([]), and the items are separated using commas (,). They are similar to the C arrays. Although all array elements must be of the same type, lists support the storage of items belonging to different types in a single list.

We use the slice operator ([ ] and [:]) for accessing the elements of a list. The indices start from 0 and end at -1. Also, the plus symbol (+) represents the concatenation operator, while the asterisk (*) represents the repetition operator. Example:

```
#!/usr/bin/python3

lst1 = [ 'joel', 3980 , 9.00, 'sister', 44.31 ]
lst2 = [102, 'sister']

# will print the complete list
print (lst1)

# will print the first element of the list
print (lst1[0])
```

```
# will print the elements starting from the 2nd
till 3rd
print (lst1[1:3])

# will print the elements starting from the 3rd
element
print (lst1[2:])

# will print the list two times
print (lst2 * 2)

# will print a concatenated lists
print (lst1 + lst2)
```

There is no much difference in what is happening in the above code compared to the previous one for strings. When executed, the program outputs:

```
['joel', 3980, 9.0, 'sister', 44.31]
joel
[3980, 9.0]
[9.0, 'sister', 44.31]
[102, 'sister', 102, 'sister']
['joel', 3980, 9.0, 'sister', 44.31, 102, 'sister']
```

In the statement "print (lst1)", we print the contents of lst1. Note that each element is treated to be at its own index as a whole, for example, element 'joel' is treated as a single element of a list at index 0.

A tuple is just a sequence data type, similar to a list. It is made up of several values that are separated by the use of commas. The tuples have to be enclosed by the use of parenthesis.

Unlike a list, the elements in a tuple cannot be changed or updated. Consider the example given below:

```
#!/usr/bin/python

tpl1 = ( 'joel', 390 , 5.20, 'sister', 96.2 )
tpl2 = (563, 'jane')

# Will print the complete tuple
print (tpl1)

# will print the first element of tuple
print (tpl1[0])

# will print the elements  from 2nd till 3rd
print (tpl1[1:3])

# will print the elements  from 3rd element
print (tpl1[2:])

# will print the list two times
print (tpl2 * 2)

# will print concatenated tuples
sprint (tpl1 + tpl2)
```

Execute the program, and you will get the following result:

```
('joel', 390, 5.2, 'sister', 96.2)
joel
(390, 5.2)
(5.2, 'sister', 96.2)
(563, 'jane', 563, 'jane')
('joel', 390, 5.2, 'sister', 96.2, 563, 'jane')
```

We can now explore the differences between lists and tuples in Python. They are closely related. Hence most people forget about their differences.

A tuple denotes an assortment of data, with the data elements being separated by commas, making it similar to a Python list. However, the difference comes in that a Python tuple is immutable. This means that you cannot modify, change or manipulate it. The use of a tuple is motivated by this property. It is mostly applied in sequence unpacking, where there is a need to keep the returned data to certain variables. Here is an example:

```
def tupleUseExample():
    return 20, 50

p, q = tupleUseExample()
print(p, q)
```

The code will return the following output upon execution:

```
20 50
```

In the example, a tuple has been used, and it cannot be modified. You have noticed that we have not added brackets around the tuple. If you don't use brackets or braces around it, Python will automatically treat it as a tuple. You can also create tuples using the curved brackets ().

When defining Python lists, we use square brackets. A Python list has a similar mode of operation, like arrays in languages such as PHP. The following example demonstrates the usage of a list in Python:

```
p = [2, 5, 7, 9, 1, 7, 3]
'''
the whole list can be referenced as:
'''
print(p)
print(p[0],p[1])
```

The code will return the following result upon execution:

```
[2, 5, 7, 9, 1, 7, 3]
2 5
```

Sometimes, we may need to change the elements which are contained in a particular list. In Python, we can update either a single or multiple elements of a list. If you need to add extra elements to your list, you have to use the *append()* method. Consider the example given below:

```
#!/usr/bin/python3

lst = ['java', 'python', 2567, 8923]

print ("The element at index 0 of the list is: ", lst[0])
print ("The element at index 1 of the list is: ", lst[1])
print ("The element at index 2 of the list is: ", lst[2])
print ("The element at index 3 of the list is: ", lst[3])
lst[2] = 5634
print ("The new value available at the index 2 after update is: ", lst[2])
```

In this example, we have accessed the elements which are in the list by use of their respective indices. At first, the element at index 2, that is, the third element in the list is 2567. Our aim is to change this value so that it can be 5634. This logic has implemented in the following line of code:

lst[2] = 5634

We have then tried to access the value, which is now located at this index, and we get 5634 as the value. This shows that our update was done successfully. When you execute the code, you should get the following result:

```
The element at index 0 of the list is:   java
The element at index 1 of the list is:   python
The element at index 2 of the list is:   2567
The element at index 3 of the list is:   8923
The new value available at the index 2 after update is:
```

Python provides us with two methods that can be used for the deletion of an element from a list. The *"del()"* function is used when we know the element which we need to delete, while the *"remove()"* method is used when we are not aware of the element which we need to remove.

Consider the example given below:

```
#!/usr/bin/python3
lst = ['java', 'python', 2567, 8923]

print (lst)
del lst[2]
print ("List elements after deleting the element at index 2 : ", lst)
```

Note that our list has four elements, and we are deleting the element located at index 2, that is, the third element in the list. We have then printed out the list after the deletion of this element. The code will return the following upon execution:

```
['java', 'python', 2567, 8923]
List elements after deleting the element at index 2 :  ['java', 'python', 8923]
```

Python Dictionaries

Python dictionaries are used for the storage of key-value pairs. With dictionaries, you can use a key to retrieve, remove, add, or modify values. Dictionaries are also mutable, meaning you can't their values once declared.

To create dictionaries, we use curly braces. Every dictionary item has a key, then followed by a colon, then a value. The items are separated using a comma (,). Example:

```
#!/usr/bin/python3
classmates = {
    'joel' : '233-181-421',
    'mercy' : '203-23-157'
}
```

We have created a dictionary named *classmates* with two items. Note that the key must be of a type that is hashable, but you may use any value. Each dictionary key must be unique. The first element, *joel,* is the key, followed by the value. In the second element, *mercy* is the element. To access dictionary elements, use the dictionary name and the key. Example:

```
#!/usr/bin/python3
classmates = {
    'joel' : '233-181-421',
    'mercy' : '203-23-157'
}
```

```
print("The number for joel is",
classmates['joel'])
print("The number for mercy is",
classmates['mercy'])
```

The last two statements help us access the dictionary values. It prints:

```
The number for joel is 233-181-421
The number for mercy is 203-23-157
```

To know the dictionary length, run the *len()* function as follows:

len(classmates)

The above will return 2 as the dictionary has only two elements.

Datatype Conversion

Python allows you to convert data from one type to another. The process of converting from one data type to another is known as *typecasting*.

If you need to convert your *int* datatype into a *float*, you call the *float()* function. Example:

```
#!/usr/bin/python3
p=15
print("The value of p in int is", p)
print("The value of p in float is", float(p))
```

In the above example, *p* has been initialized to 15. We have called the *float()* function and passed *p* to it as the parameter. The integer value, that is, 15 has been converted into a float value, that is, 15.0. The program prints the following:

```
The value of p in int is 15
The value of p in float is 15.0
```

To convert a float into an int, you call the *int()* function. Example:

```
#!/usr/bin/python3
p=15.0
print("The value of p in float is", p)
print("The value of p in int is", int(p))
```

The program prints the following:

```
The value of p in float is 15.0
The value of p in int is 15
```

We have called the *int()* function and passed the parameter *p* to it. It has converted 15.0 to 15, which is a float-to-integer conversion.

If you need to convert a number to a string, you call the *str()* function. The number will then be converted into a string. Example:

```
#!/usr/bin/python3

x=20
print("The value of x in int is", x)
```

```
print("The value of x in string is", str(x))
```

The program outputs:

```
The value of x in int is 20
The value of x in string is 20
```

Although the value is the same, it is treated differently by the Python interpreter. The conversion of a float to a string can also be done similarly.

Chapter 3- Python Operators

Operators are constructs that can be used for manipulation of operand values.

Consider the expression 1 + 7 = 8. In this expression, the plus symbol (+) is the operator, while the 1 and 7 are operands.

Let us discuss some of the operators which are supported in Python.

Arithmetic Operators

These include the following:

- Addition (+)
- Subtraction (-)
- Multiplication (*)
- Division (/)
- Modulus (%)- returns the remainder after division.
- Exponent (**)- performs an exponential (power) calculation

Consider the example given below:

```
#!/usr/bin/python

x = 17
y = 4
```

```
z = 0
z = x + y
print("x + y= ", z)

z = x - y
print("x - y =", z)

z = x * y
print ("x * y =", z)

z = x / y
print ("z = x / y ", z)

z = x % y
print ("x % y = ", z)

x = 2
y = 4
z = x**y
print ("x**y = ", z)

x = 10
y = 5
z = x//y
print ("x//y = ", z)
```

The program should give you the following result:

```
x + y=   21
x - y = 13
x * y = 68
z = x / y   4.25
x % y =   1
x**y =   16
x//y =   2
```

You might be familiar with some of the above operators, but some be challenging to you. In "z = x % y" expression, we get the remainder after dividing "x" by "y". The value of x is 17, and y is 4. 4 goes into 17 four times to give 16, and the remainder is 1. This is why the result for that operation is 1.

In (x**y), we are raising x to the power of y, which is x^y. The value of x is 2, while that of y is 4, giving us 2^4, and the result is 16, explaining the source of result 16.

Comparison Operators

These operators work by comparing the values on either side, and then they return the relationship between them. They include the following:

- == equal to
- != not equal to
- <>Similar to !=
- \> greater than
- < less than
- \>= greater than or equal to
- <= less than or equal to

Consider the following example:

```
#!/usr/bin/python

x = 12
y = 6
```

```
z = 0

if ( x == y ):
   print ("x == y is True")
else:
   print ("x == y is False")

if ( x != y ):
   print ("x != y is True")
else:
   print ("x != y is False")

if ( x < y ):
   print ("x < y is True")
else:
   print ("x <= y is False")

if ( x > y ):
   print ("x > y is True")
else:
   print ("x > y is False")

x = 5;
y = 20;
if ( x <= y ):
   print ("x <= y is True")
else:
   print ("x <= y is False")

if ( y >= x ):
   print ("x >= y is True")
else:
   print ("x >= y is False")
```

Execution of the program will give you the following result:

```
x == y is False
x != y is True
x <= y is False
x > y is True
x <= y is True
x >= y is True
```

Chapter 4- Flow Control

Python provides us with constructs and statements that we can use to control how the execution of programs flows. The goal in flow-control is to evaluate an expression or expressions, then determine the action to perform depending on whether the expression is TRUE or FALSE.

Let us discuss the various statements that can be used for flow control in Python:

The "if" statement

This statement is made up of a logical expression that has to be evaluated first, and then the action taken will be based on the final decision. It takes the syntax given below:

```
if expression:
   statement(s)
```

The Python interpreter will first evaluate the expression in the "*if*" statement. If this expression is found to be true, then the statements which are below the "*if*" are executed. In case the expression evaluates to a false, then the set of statements that are located immediately after the loop will be executed. Note that after the ":", statements should be indented to the same level since they belong to a similar block.

Example:

```
#!/usr/bin/python3
age = 32
if age==32:
    print ("You are not much old")
    print ("You are",age, "years")

weight = 77
if weight<=60:
    print ("your weight is not that bad!")
    print ("Your weight is", weight, "kilograms")
print ("Thank you!")
```

The code returns the following upon execution:

```
You are not much old
You are 32 years
Thank you!
```

As shown in the program, we first set the value of age to 32. The first "*if*" statement tests whether the value of age is 32, and since this is true, the print statement below it was executed. The value has then been set to 77. The second "*if*" statement evaluates to a true since its value is less than 60. This is why the print statement below it was executed.

Suppose the first "*if*" statement evaluates to a false. Consider the code given below for the same program after modification:

```
#!/usr/bin/python3
age = 32
```

```
if age==30:
    print ("You are not much old")
    print ("You are",age, "years")

weight = 77
if weight<=80:
    print ("your weight is not that bad!")
    print ("Your weight is", weight, "kilograms")
print ("Thank you!")
```

The code returns the following:

```
your weight is not that bad!
Your weight is 77 kilograms
Thank you!
```

The value of age has been set to 32. We are testing whether this value is equal to 30, which will evaluate to false. The print statements below this expression should be skipped.

The second "*if*" evaluates to true, and the *print* statements within its block are executed, giving the above result. Consider the code given below:

```
#!/usr/bin/python3

age = 32
if age==32:
    print ("You are not much old")
    print ("You are",age, "years")

weight = 77
if weight<=60:
```

```
    print ("your weight is not that bad!")
    print ("Your weight is", weight, "kilograms")
print ("Thank you!")
```

The code will return the following result:

```
        You are not much old
        You are 32 years
        Thank you!
```

The second "*if*" evaluated to false, and the *print* statements within its block were skipped. Note that the last print statement with the "*Thank you!*" message will be evaluated whether or not any of the "*if*" statements are true or not.

The "if...elif...else" statement

It is possible for us to combine an "*if*" statement with an "*else*" part in Python. If the "*if*" expression evaluates to a true, then its part is executed, but in case it evaluates to a false, then the part for "*else*" will be executed. Note that an "*if*" statement should be followed by at most one "*else*" statement. This statement takes the following syntax:

```
if expression:
    statement(s)
else:
    statement(s)
```

Consider the example given below, which shows how this statement can be used in Python:

```
#!/usr/bin/python3
price=2000
if price<1500:
    discount=price*0.05
    print ("The product discount is",discount)
else:
    discount=price*0.10
    print ("The product discount is",discount)

print ("You should pay:",price-discount,"for the product")
```

In this example, we have a variable named *price* with a value of 2000. We have then used the "*if*" statement to check for the range of the price, that is, whether it is less than 1500. If this is the case, the discount on the product is 0.05 multiplied by the price of the product. The "*else*" part is the default one when the condition for the "*if*" expression evaluates to a false, that is when the price of the product is greater than 1500. The price is 2000, so the "*else*" part will run.

The code returns the following output:

```
The product discount is 200.0
You should pay: 1800.0 for the product
```

The discount in this example was obtained by multiplying the price, which is 2000 by 0.10 as specified in the "*else*" part. That is how this statement can be used in Python.

The "elif" Statement

This statement is used when there are multiple expressions which are to be executed, and a particular block of code is executed once an expression evaluates to a TRUE. Note that the statement is optional. This is also the case with the "*else*" statement. The difference comes in that for the case of the "*else*" statement, there can be at most one statement, but in this case, we can have any arbitrary number of statements that follow the "*if*" statement. This statement takes the following syntax:

```
if expressiona:
    statement(s)
elif expressionb:
    statement(s)
elif expressionc:
    statement(s)
else:
    statement(s)
```

This is a very powerful statement. It can be used to substitute the switch or the case statement, which is used in the other programming languages.

```
#!/usr/bin/python3
price=2000
```

```
if price<1500:
    discount=price*0.05
    print ("The product discount is:",discount)
elif price<5000:
    discount=price*0.10
    print ("The product discount is:",discount)
else:
    discount=price*0.15
    print ("The product discount is:",discount)

print ("You should pay:",price-discount,"for the product")
```

Again, we have set the price of the product to be 2000. The expression for "*if price<5000:*" will evaluate to a true as this is where the value of price lies. The discount will be calculated using the formula "*discount=price*0.10*".

That is how this statement can be used. Note that in Python, you don't have to use the *AND* (&&) or the *OR* (||) operator like in the other programming languages such as Java. If it was the case with Java, the statement "*if price<5000:*" would have been written as "*if (price>1500&& price<5000)*"so that we can evaluate whether the value of price lies between 1500 and 5000. Python takes care of this as we had first determined whether the price is less than 1500.

The Nested "if"

In some situations, you may be in need of evaluating a certain condition in case the one you are evaluating becomes true. We can use a nested *"if"* statement.

It is also possible for us to nest an *"if...elif...else"* statement. The nesting takes the syntax given below:

```
if expressiona:
    statement
    if expressionb:
        statement
    elif expressionc:
        statement
    else
        statement
elif expressiond:
    statement
else:
    statement
```

The following example demonstrates how nesting of decision-making statements can be done in Python:

```
# !/usr/bin/python3
price=2000
if price<3000:
    if price==2000:
        print ("The product price is below 3000. It is 2000")
    else:
        print ("The product price is below 3000 but not 2000")
```

```
else:
    if price<5000:
        print ("The product price is below 5000")
    else:
        print  ("The product price is above 5000")
```

The price is 2000. The expression "*if price<3000:*" will evaluate to a true. The nested expression "*if price==2000:*" will also evaluate to a true. The code will return the following upon execution:

```
The product price is below 3000. It is 2000
```

Chapter 5- Loops and Control Statements

With Python loops, we can specify the number of times that we need to execute a particular section of code. Let us discuss the various loops supported in Python:

For Loop

This loop is used for iterating over something. It will perform something based on each item in the block. The loop is the best if you are aware of the number of times you need the task to be executed.

"RANGE()" function

This function is used when we need to iterate through a sequence of numbers that we specify. The result of the function is an iterator for arithmetic progressions. Open the Python terminal then type the following:

```
>>> list(range(15))
[0, 1, 2, 3, 4, 5, 6, 7, 8, 9, 10, 11, 12, 13, 14]
>>>
```

As shown above, when you list *range(15)*, it will print the values between 0 and 15, with 15 excluded. If the number specified is *n*, then the function usually returns up to *n-1* items, meaning that the list's last item is not included. This can be combined with *for* loop. Example:

```
#!/usr/bin/python3

for p in list(range(15)):
    print (p)
```

The code outputs:

```
0
1
2
3
4
5
6
7
8
9
10
11
12
13
14
```

Although 15 is the range specified, it is not included in result.

Note that other than combining *for* loop with *range()* function, it can be used alone. In such a case, you can iterate thought items with the loop. Example, you can iterate through elements of a list with *for* loop:

```
#!/usr/bin/python3

lst = [12,20,35,49]

for p in lst:
    print(p)
```

We created the list named *ls1* with 4 elements. The *for* loop has been used for iterating through these elements. The code prints the following:

```
12
20
35
49
```

A for loop involves the definition of a parameter that will be used for purposes of iteration through elements. In the above example, the variable *p* has been defined and used for iterating through list elements.

The *Range()* function makes the tasks of specifying the range to be executed very easily. You can use the syntax given below:

```
range(a,b)
```

The above function will execute and print items between a and b. Practically, consider the example given below:

```
#!/usr/bin/python3

for p in range(20, 29):
    print(p)
```

The code prints:

```
20
21
22
23
24
25
26
27
28
```

The code printed values between 20 and 29. Although 20 is included, 29 is not included.

This means the initial value is included, while the last value is excluded.

Also, the range () function takes another parameter that allows us to specify the steps by which an increment is to be done. Example:

```
#!/usr/bin/python3

for p in range(5, 15, 2):
    print(p)
```

The code prints the following:

```
5
7
9
11
13
```

We are printing between 5 and 15, and each iteration will be incremented by 2. Note that 15 is not part of the output.

The *for* loop may also be combined with *else* part. Example:

```
#!/usr/bin/python3

values = [7,41,22,38,37,75,90,11,62,73,42]

for p in values:
   if p%2 == 0:
      print ('Even numbers detected!')
      break
else:
   print ('No even numbers detected!')
```

The code will print:

```
Even numbers detected!
```

We used the modulus (%) operator to check whether there are even numbers. The operator returns the remainder after division. If there are numbers in the list in which we remain with 0 after dividing by 2, then the list has some even numbers. Try to create the list without even numbers and see the *else* part will run:

```
#!/usr/bin/python3

values = [7,41,21,39,37,75,91,11,61,73,43]

for p in values:
   if p%2 == 0:
      print ('Even numbers detected!')
      break
```

```
else:
    print ('No even numbers detected!')
```
The code will print:

```
No even numbers detected!
```

While Loop

In a *while* loop, we specify a condition to be evaluated after every iteration, and the code will always run provided the condition is true. The execution of code halts immediately if the condition becomes false. The loop evaluates the condition after every iteration, and the moment it finds itself violating the loop condition, it stops execution of the code. Example:

```
#!/usr/bin/python3

val = 87

while val < 100:
    print("Val is", val)
    val += 1
```

The value of variable *var* was initialized to 87. The *while* condition tests whether this value is below 100. As long as the value of *val* is less than 100, the loop will be executed. The code prints:

```
Val is 87
Val is 88
Val is 89
Val is 90
Val is 91
Val is 92
Val is 93
Val is 94
Val is 95
Val is 96
Val is 97
Val is 98
Val is 99
```

As shown, the code counted until the value of *val* was 99. When it reached 100, it found itself violating the loop condition, that is, the number must be less than 100. The execution stopped immediately.

Note that 100 is not part of the output. To include it, we can use *less than or equal to* sign (<=) as shown below:

```
#!/usr/bin/python3

val = 87

while val <= 100:
    print("Val is", val)
    val += 1
```

The code prints the following:

```
Val is 87
Val is 88
Val is 89
Val is 90
Val is 91
Val is 92
Val is 93
Val is 94
Val is 95
Val is 96
Val is 97
Val is 98
Val is 99
Val is 100
```

The use of the symbol has included 100 in the output. However, the execution of the program cannot go past that, but it halts immediately if it finds itself violating the loop condition. Another example:

```
#!/usr/bin/python3

age = 58
while (age < 60):
    print ("You have not reached retirement age. Your age is", age)
    age = age + 1

print ("Prepare yourself for retirement.")
```

The code returns the following output:

```
You have not reached retirement age. Your age is 58
You have not reached retirement age. Your age is 59
Prepare yourself for retirement.
```

We have specified a default statement to run when the loop condition becomes *false*.

Loop Control

It's possible to change the normal execution of a loop to something else. This can be done using some statements. Once execution has left scope, the objects within that scope will be destroyed. Python supports a number of loop control statements:

break Statement

This statement helps us terminate the execution of a loop prematurely. The execution then begins at the next statement after the loop. It's similar to *break* statement in C. When executing a loop, an external condition may arise that may require instant termination of the loop. The *break* statement can help you in this case. The statement can be used both with *for* and *while* loop. Example:

```
#!/usr/bin/python3

# Example 1
for letter in 'Georgia':
   if letter == 'r':
      break
   print ('Current letter is :', letter)

# Example 2
```

```
x = 5
while x > 0:
    print ('Current variable value :', x)
    x = x -1
    if x == 2:
        break

print ("The End!")
```

The code prints:

```
Current letter is : G
Current letter is : e
Current letter is : o
Current variable value : 5
Current variable value : 4
Current variable value : 3
The End!
```

First, the loop is iterating through the letters of name *Georgia*. Once it encounters letter *r*, it should break or halt iterating through the name letters. In the second example, we are iterating through numbers 5 downwards to 0. When the loop encounters 2, it should break as specified in the condition. Example 2:

In this example, we will be searching through elements of a list. The user is prompted to enter a number which, if found, the user will get *found* message. If not, the user will get the *not found* message:

```
#!/usr/bin/python3
userInput= int(input('Which number do you want to search? '))
```

```
lst = [10,22,45,40,13,9,8,7,68,28,90]

for p in lst:
   if p == userInput:
      print ('Number found')
      break
else:
   print ('Number not found')
```

After running the code, search for number 68. You will get this:

```
Which number do you want to search? 68
Number found
```

It's true number 68 is in the list. Search for a number which is not part of the list. Observe the result:

```
Which number do you want to search? 1000
Number not found
```

continue Statement

With this statement, execution is returned to the start of the current loop. Once a loop encounters it, it will begin the next iteration and leave remaining statements in the current iteration. It is applicable to both *while* and *for* loops. Example:

```
#!/usr/bin/python3

# Example 1
for letter in 'Georgia':
```

```
    if letter == 'r':
        continue
    print ('Current letter is :', letter)

# Example 2
x = 5
while x > 0:
    x = x -1
    if x == 2:
        continue
    print ('Current variable value is :', x)


print ("The End!")
```

The code prints the following after execution:

```
Current letter is : G
Current letter is : e
Current letter is : o
Current letter is : g
Current letter is : i
Current letter is : a
Current variable value is : 4
Current variable value is : 3
Current variable value is : 1
Current variable value is : 0
The End!
```

What happened is that the interpreter skipped *r* in the first example and 2 in the second example. This is different from the *break* statement.

pass Statement

This statement is applicable where a statement is needed syntactically, but you don't want to execute any statement on that part. It can be seen as *null* operation as nothing happens after it's executed. Example:

```
#!/usr/bin/python3

for letter in 'Georgia':
   if letter == 'r':
      pass
      print ('The pass block')
   print ('The current letter is :', letter)

print ("The End!")
```

The code gives the following when executed:

```
The current letter is : G
The current letter is : e
The current letter is : o
The pass block
The current letter is : r
The current letter is : g
The current letter is : i
The current letter is : a
The End!
```

The code just skipped, but execution resumed to normal after that. You notice that the letter *r* is now part of the output. This is not what happened in the previous two statements.

Chapter 6- Functions

The purpose of functions is to group related code together. Such code can then be used to perform a single function. Functions enhance the modularity of your code, and at the same time, they promote code reuse.

It is true that Python comes with many inbuilt functions, but it is possible for you to create your own functions. The functions that you create will be referred to as *user-defined functions*.

Defining Functions

Functions can be defined so that we can get the functionality that we require. To define a function, we use the *"def"* keyword, then the function name, and then the parenthesis (()).

The parameters or the input arguments have to be placed inside the parenthesis. The parameters can also be defined within parenthesis. The function has a body or the code block, and this must begin with a colon (:) and it has to be indented. In Python, the definition of functions takes the following syntax:

```
def function_name( arguments ):
   "function_docstring"
   function_suite
   return [expression]
```

Note that the default setting is that arguments have a positional behavior. This means that they should be passed while following the order in which you defined them.

Example:

```
#!/usr/bin/python3

def aFunction():
    print('The function code to run')
    p = 19 + 12
    print(p)
```

We have defined a function named *aFunction*. The parameters of a function are like the variables for the function. The parameters are usually added inside the parenthesis, but our above function has no parameters. When you run the above code, nothing will happen since we simply defined the function and specified what it should do. The function can be called as shown below:

```
#!/usr/bin/python3

def aFunction():
    print('The function code to run')
    p = 19 + 12
    print(p)
aFunction()
```

It will print this:

```
The function code to run
31
```

That is how we can have a basic Python function.

Function Parameters

You can dynamically define arguments for a function. Example:

```
#!/usr/bin/python3

def getSum(p, q):
    result = p + q
    print('The first number is', p)
    print('The second number is', q)
    print("The sum is", result)

getSum(19,10)
```

The code returns the following result:

```
The first number is 19
The second number is 10
The sum is 29
```

We defined a function named *getSum*. The function takes two parameters, namely *p* and *q*. We have another variable named *result,* which is the sum of the two function parameters. In the last statement, we have called the function and passed the values for the two parameters. The function will calculate the value of the variable *result* by adding the two numbers. We finally get the result shown above.

Note that during our function definition, we specified two parameters, p and q. Try to call the function will either more than two parameters or 1 parameter and see what happens. Example:

```
#!/usr/bin/python3

def getSum(p, q):
    result = p + q
    print('The first number is', p)
    print('The second number is', q)
    print("The sum is", result)
```

getSum(19)

In the last statement in our code above, we have passed only one argument to the function, that is, 19. The program gives an error when executed:

```
Traceback (most recent call last):
  File "C:/Users/admin/var.py", line 9, in <module>
    getSum(19)
TypeError: getSum() missing 1 required positional argument: 'q'
```

The error message simply tells us one argument is missing. What if we run it with more than two arguments:

```
#!/usr/bin/python3
```

```
def getSum(p, q):
    result = p + q
    print('The first number is', p)
    print('The second number is', q)
    print("The sum is", result)

getSum(19, 10, 3)
```

We also get an error message:

```
Traceback (most recent call last):
  File "C:/Users/admin/var.py", line 9, in <module>
    getSum(19, 10, 3)
TypeError: getSum() takes 2 positional arguments but 3 were given
```

The error message tells us the function expects two arguments but we have passed 3 to it.

In most programming languages, parameters to a function can be passed either by reference or by value. Python supports parameter passing only by reference. This means if what the parameter refers to is changed in the function, the same change will also be reflected in the calling function. Example:

```
#!/usr/bin/python3

def referencePass(lst):
    print ("List values before change: ", lst)
    lst[0]=1200
    print ("List values after change: ", lst)
    return

# Calling the function
lst = [1150,2345,6776]
```

```
referencePass( lst )
print ("Values outside function: ", lst)
```

The code gives this result:

```
List values before change:  [1150, 2345, 6776]
List values after change:   [1200, 2345, 6776]
Values outside function:    [1200, 2345, 6776]
```

What we have done in this example is that we have maintained the reference of the objects which are being passed and then values have been appended to the same function.

In the next example below, we are passing by reference then the same reference will be overwritten inside the same function which has been called:

```
#!/usr/bin/python3

def referencePass( lst ):
   lst = [10,22,35,49]
   print ("Values inside the function: ", lst)
   return

lst = [53,101,87]
referencePass( lst )
print ("Values outside function: ", lst)
```

The code gives this result:

```
Values inside the function:  [10, 22, 35, 49]
Values outside function:     [53, 101, 87]
```

Note that the "lst" parameter will be local to the function "referencePass". Even if this is changed within the function, the "lst" will not be affected in any way. As the output shows above, the function helps us achieve nothing.

Function Parameter Defaults

There are default parameters for functions, which the function creator can use in his or her functions. This means that one has the choice of using the default parameters or even using the ones they need to use by specifying them. To use the default parameters, the parameters having defaults are expected to be the last ones written in function parameters. Example:

```
#!/usr/bin/python3

def (p, q=13):
    pass
```

In the above example, the parameter q has been given a default value, unlike parameter p. The parameter q has been written as the last one in the function parameters. The values for such a function may be accessed as follows:

```
#!/usr/bin/python3

def myFunction(p,q,r='XYZ'):
    # printing everything
```

```
    print(p,q,r)
myFunction(280,266)
```

The code outputs the following:

```
280 266 XYZ
```

The parameter *r* had been given a default value, that is, XYZ. In the last line of the above code, we have passed only two parameters to the function, that is, the values for p and q parameters. However, after calling the function, it returned the values for the three parameters. This means for a parameter with default, we don't need to specify its value or even mention it when calling the function.

However, it's still possible for you to specify the value for the parameter during the function call. You can specify a different value to what had been specified as the default and you will get the new one as value of the parameter. Example:

```
#!/usr/bin/python3

def myFunction(p,q,r='XYZ'):
    # printing everything
    print(p,q,r)
myFunction(280,266,'ABC')
```

The program outputs this:

```
280 266 ABC
```

Above, the value for a parameter was given the default value "XYZ". When calling the function in the last line of the code, we specified a different value for this parameter, which is "ABC". The code returned the value as "ABC". The default value was overridden.

An Anonymous Function

These are the types of functions that we don't need to use the "*def*" keyword so as to define them. Some small anonymous functions can be declared by the use of the "*lambda*" keyword. Such a function can take as many arguments as possible, and it may give you a single value in return.

In Python, lambda functions take the syntax given below:

```
lambda [arg1 [,arg2,.....argn]]:expression
```

Consider the example given below showing how such functions can be used in Python:

```
#!/usr/bin/python3

#Let us define our function
getSum = lambda p, q: p + q

# Let us call our function
```

```
print ("The value after addition is : ", getSum(
10, 29))
print ("The value after addition is : ", getSum(
13, 17 ))
```

The code returns the following:

```
The value after addition is :   39
The value after addition is :   30
```

Note that we have defined a lambda function, which is expected to take two arguments that is: *p* and *q*. These two arguments are to be added so that we can get the value for "*getSum*". We have lastly called our function twice, in which case, two arguments have been passed to the function in each call. These two have been added to get the value of "*getSum*".

The "return" Statement

When this statement is used, it causes the Python interpreter to exit a function, and it will then pass an expression to the caller, which is optional. If a return statement is used without arguments, it is like telling it to return nothing. In our previous functions, we have not returned anything.

Consider the example given below, which shows how we can return from a function:

```
#!/usr/bin/python3
```

```
# Let us define our function
def getSum( p, q ):
    # addding our parameters and then returning the result"
    result = p + q
    print ("We have the following inside the function : ", result)
    return result

# Let us call our function
result = getSum( 10, 19 )
print ("We have the following outside the function : ", result )
```

The code returns the following result:

```
We have the following inside the function :  29
We have the following outside the function :  29
```

Note that we defined the function taking two arguments. The variable "*result*" has been defined, and this should be the result after adding the two integers. Our return statement takes this variable, meaning that our function should return "*result*". That is how the return statement is used in Python.

The Variable Scope

Once you have declared a variable, it may not be possible for you to access it from anywhere within the program. Variable accessibility depends on the location you have declared it. The following are the two basic scopes in Python:

1. Global scope
2. Local Scope

A variable is said to have a local scope if it is defined within a particular function, while a function defined outside a function is said to have a global scope.

With this, local variables are only accessible within the function they have been defined, but the global variables can be accessed from any part of the program. Any function within the program is capable of accessing a global variable. After a function has been made, all the variables declared in it will be brought into scope. This means that they will be accessible from the region you have called the function.

Consider the example given below:

```
#!/usr/bin/python3

result = 0 # This is a global variable.
# Let us define our function
def getSum( p, q ):
    # Let us add the parameters and then return teh result."
    result = p + q; # This is a local variable.
    print ("The local total inside the function is : ", result)
    return result
```

```
# Let us call our function
getSum( 10, 19 )
print ("The global total outside the function is
: ", result )
```

The code returns the following output:

```
The local total inside the function is :   29
The global total outside the function is :   0
```

We defined a variable named *"result"* with 0 as its value. We have then defined a variable named *"getSum"* to take two arguments. Inside this function, we have defined the value of sum to be the result of the addition of the two arguments to the function. The first print statement is inside this function, so it has access to this logic. The second print statement is outside the function, meaning that it will have no access to this logic.

When we call the function as done in the line *"getSum(10,19)"*, the first print statement will have access to *"result = p + q;"*, so it will add 10 and 19 to get 29. The second print statement does not have access to the above logic. Hence it will access the initial declaration that *"result=0"*.

Chapter 7- Error and Exception Handling

When writing and executing our Python code, errors and exceptions may occur. That is why we should add a mechanism within our code that will help us deal with this. With error and exception handling, we are able to detect errors and handle them appropriately. If you are searching for a file and it is not found, for example, you can raise an error message. The *try* and except statements are used in Python for error handling. These statements follow the same concept followed in the *if-else* statement, in which if the *if* part runs, the *else* part will not run. Consequently, if the *try* part runs, the *except* part won't run. If the *try* part fails, then the exception part will run with error generated in *try* part. With exception handling, your code can be kept running even in cases when it could have failed. Error handling is also a good way of logging any problems that you may have in your code. You may also correct the problem with your code.

The syntax for *try-and-except* is:

```
try:
    # Your code
    # to throw an exception
except <ExceptionType>:
    # exception handling for alerting the user
```

To see it work, you only have to write the code that will throw an exception. In case of the occurrence of an exception, the *try* code will be skipped. If you have a matching exception in *except* part, then it will be executed to handle the exception. Consider the following example:

```
# import module sys for returning exception type
import sys

aList = ['x', 0, 4]

for divVal in aList:
    try:
        print("The division value is", divVal)
        result = 1/int(divVal)
        break
    except:
        print("Oooops!",sys.exc_info()[0],"occured.")
        print("Next entry.")
        print()
print("The result after dividing by",divVal,"is",result)
```

The code will return the following upon execution:

```
The division value is x
Oooops! <class 'ValueError'> occured.
Next entry.

The division value is 0
Oooops! <class 'ZeroDivisionError'> occured
Next entry.

The division value is 4
The result after dividing by 4 is 0.25
```

What we are doing in the above example is that we are dividing 1 by three values that we have passed within a Python list. A division by value x resulted in an exception, and we are able to tell the name of the exception as ValueError. A division by 0 also resulted in an exception, and we are able to tell its name as "ZeroDivisionError". However, a division by 4 ran successfully. Note that the various types of exceptions are defined in the sys library. Hence we imported it.

In case no exception had occurred, the *except* block would have been skipped, and a normal flow of execution would have continued. However, anytime an exception occurs, the *except* block has to catch it, as shown in the above case. Here is another simple example:

```
#!/usr/bin/python3

try:
    myfile = open('classnames.txt', 'r')
    print(myfile.read())
```

```
    myfile.close()
except IOError:
    print('The file was not found')
```

The code will print the following:

```
The file was not found
```

We are trying to access a file and read it. That is in the *try* statement. However, in the *except* part, we have the *IOError*, which handles input/output exceptions. We have defined what should happen in case of such an occurrence, that is if the file is not found. It should execute the *print* statement. Just run the code and ensure you don't have the file. The *print* statement will be printed.

If the file is found, then the part under *except* statement will be skipped. In my case, the exception occurred. Hence the *try* part was skipped, that is, the file was not read. For the *except the* part to run, the exception that occurs must match the one you are handling. Note that our code given above is only capable of handling the "IOError" exception. To handle ay more errors, we should add other *except* clauses. This means that we may have numerous *except* clauses in a single *try* clause, as well as an optional *else* or finally clause.

Raising Exceptions

In Python, we raise exceptions after the occurrence of their corresponding errors during runtime. The exceptions can be raised forcefully by the use of the *raise* keyword. A value can also be passed to an exception so as to tell the reason behind raising of the exception:

The *raise* keyword can be used, as shown below:

```
raise ExceptionClass("An argument")
```

Here is an example:

```
#!/usr/bin/python3

def yourValue(x):
   if x < 0:
      raise ValueError("Value MUST be a positive integer value")

   if x % 2 == 1:
      print("An odd number detected")
   else:
      print("An even number detected")

   try:
      p = int(input("Enter a number "))
      yourValue(p)

   except ValueError:
      print("Only positive integers are allowed")
```

```
except:
    print("something went wrong")
```

Run the code and enter a number. In my case, I have entered an odd number, and I got the following result:

```
Enter a number 9
An odd number detected
```

When 9 is divided by 2, the remainder is a 1. Hence the code was able to tell it is an odd number. Enter an even number and see the result that you get:

```
Enter a number 10
An even number detected
```

Now, enter a negative number and see the result that you get. It should be as follows:

```
Enter a number -1
Only positive integers are allowed
```

That is how you can raise exceptions on your methods.

Exception Objects

Now that you are familiar with handling exceptions in Python, let us learn how to access the exception object in the code for the exception handler. The following code may be used for assigning a variable to an exception object. The following syntax should be used for this:

```
try:
    # code for throwing an exception
except TypeOfException as ex:
    # code for handling the exception
```

The exception object can be stored in the variable *ex*. The exception can then be used in the exception handling code. Example:

```
#!/usr/bin/python3

try:
    p = eval(input("Enter an integer value: "))
    print("The value you entered is ", p)
except NameError as ex:
    print("Exception:", ex)
```

Run the code then type a number when prompted to do so. You will get the following:

```
Enter an integer value: 3
The value you entered is  3
```

As shown above, the code executed correctly. Now, run the code then enter a string:

```
Enter an integer value: cow
Exception: name 'cow' is not defined
```

As shown above, entering a string raises an exception. This is because the code expected you to enter a number, but you have entered a string. This raises an error.

Custom Exception Class

It is possible for you to create some custom exception class. This requires you to extend the *BaseException* class or a subclass of the *BaseException* class. The *BaseException* class can be seen as the root of all the exception classes in Python.

In your text editor, create a new file named *NegativeValueException.py* then add the following code to it:

```
class NegativeValueException(RuntimeError):
    def __init__(self, yourValue):
        super().__init__()
        self.yourValue = yourValue
```

What the code does is that it creates a new exception class named *NegativeValueException*. The class has only one constructor that will call the parent class constructor by use of *super().__init__()* then set the value of *yourValue* argument. The custom exception class can be used as follows:

```
#!/usr/bin/python3

def getValue(yourValue):
    if yourValue < 0:
        raise NegativeValueException("Value MUST be a positive integer")

    if yourValue % 2 == 0:
```

```
      print("The value is an even number")
   else:
     print("The value is an odd number")

   try:
      v = int(input("Enter a value "))
      getValue(v)
   except NegativeValueException:
      print("Enter a positive integer")
   except:
      print("something went wrong")
```

You can run the code and enter a numeric value, a positive one. You will get this:

```
Enter a value 7
The value is an odd number
```

The code runs correctly. Now run the code then enter a negative integer as the value for value:

```
Enter a value -1
Traceback (most recent call last):
   File "C:\Users\admin\lsvsts.py", line 14, in <module>
     getValue(v)
   File "C:\Users\admin\lsvsts.py", line 5, in getValue
     raise NegativeValueException("Value MUST be a posit
NameError: name 'NegativeValueException' is not defined

During handling of the above exception, another excepti

Traceback (most recent call last):
   File "C:\Users\admin\lsvsts.py", line 15, in <module>
     except NegativeValueException:
NameError: name 'NegativeValueException' is not defined
```

The exception will be raised as shown above.

Let us create an exception related to *RuntimeError*. We will create a class to be a subclass of *RuntimeError* class. It is a good way of getting more information after the occurrence of an exception. The exception is raised in the *try* block then handled in the *except* block. We will use the variable *ex* for creation of an instance of class *Networkerror*:

```
class Networkerror(RuntimeError):
    def __init__(self, argu):
        self.args = argu
```

After defining the class as above, the exception can be raised as follows:

```
try:
    raise Networkerror("Wrong hostname")
except Networkerror,ex:
    print ex.args
```

Chapter 8- Working with Files

Python is a good tool for data processing. You should know to work with files in Python. Some of the file formats which can be used in Python include comma-separated values (CSV), HTML, text and JavaScript Object Notation (JSON).

Before you can write to or read from a file, you should first open it by use of *open()* function. The method works by creating a file object, which can then be used for calling other methods that are supported.

Opening and Closing Files

For a file to be read, written to, or even modified, it must first be opened. This is done using the Python in-built function named *open()*. When invoked, the function will create *file* objects that can be used for calling support methods associated with it. Here is the method's syntax:

```
file objectName = open(file_name [
,access_mode][ ,buffering])
```

The *file_name* is a string representing the name of the file to be opened. For the *access_mode*, the file can be opened for *read*, *write* or *append*. The default mode for opening a file into is *read (r)*. If the value for buffering is set to 0, then no buffering will be done. If it is set to 1, line buffering will be done after accessing the file. If you specify another integer greater than 1 for buffering, then buffering will be done at the size that you have specified. The integer is normally taken as buffer size. If it is set to a negative integer, the default buffering size for the system is used.

There are different modes in which the file may be opened. They include:

- r- the file is opened for reading only, and it's the default mode. The file pointer is placed at the start of the file.
- rb- the file is opened I binary format for reading only. The file pointer is placed at the start of the file.
- r+- the file is opened for both reading and writing. The file pointer is placed at the start of the file.
- rb+- the file is opened in binary format for reading and writing. The file pointer is placed at the start of the file.
- w- the file is opened for writing only. If the file exists, it is overwritten. If the file does not exist, a new one is created.
- wb- the file is opened in binary format for writing only. If the file exists, it is overwritten. If the file doesn't exist, a new one is created for both reading and writing.

- wb+- the file is opened in binary format for both reading and writing. If the file exists, it is overwritten. If the file doesn't exist, a new one is created.
- a- the file is opened for appending. If the file exists, the file pointer is placed at the end of the file. If the file doesn't exist, a new one is created for writing.
- ab- the file is opened in binary format for appending.
- a+- the file is opened for both reading and appending. If the file exists, the pointer is moved to the end of the file. This puts the file in the append mode. If the file doesn't exist, a new one is created for writing and reading.
- ab+- the file is opened in binary format for both reading and appending. If the file exists, the pointer is placed at the end of the file. The file is kept in append mode. If the file doesn't exist, a new one is created for writing and reading.

The file object is related to these attributes:

- file.closed- it will return *true* if the file is closed, and *false* otherwise.
- file.mode- this returns the mode in which the file is opened.
- file.name- this will return the file name.

Here is an example:

```
#!/usr/bin/python3

# Opening the file
p = open("friends.txt", "wb")
print ("The file name is: ", p.name)
print ("File closed? ", p.closed)
print ("The mode of the file? ", p.mode)

# close the file
p.close()
```

You should have a file named *friends.txt* in the directory you have saved the file with the above script. On running the code, I get the following output:

```
The file name is:  friends.txt
File closed?  False
The mode of the file?  wb
```

We have the name of the file, which was obtained by calling the *name* attribute. The *false* in the result tells us that the file is not closed. Also, it is clear that the file has been opened in binary format for writing.

To close the file, you should call the *close()* method. This method should be called for closing a file. It first flushes the unwritten information then closes the file. Once the file has been closed, no further writing can be done. If the reference object for the file is assigned to some other object, Python will automatically close the file. Whenever you need to close a file, call the *close()* method. The method syntax is as follows:

fileObject.close();

Example:

```
#!/usr/bin/python3

# Opening the file
p = open("friends.txt", "wb")
print ("The file name is :", p.name)

# Close the opened file
p.close()

print("File closed? ", p.closed)
```

Run the code in the directory with the file *friends.txt* and the following result will be printed:

```
The file name is : friends.txt
File closed?  True
```

In our previous example, we got *FALSE* when we called the *p.closed* property. This meant that the file was not closed. The reason is that we had not called the *close()* method. In the above example, we have called *close()* method on our file object. This closed the file. Hence we get *True* after calling the *p.closed* property. This means that the file has been closed.

Reading from Files

The *read()* method helps us read a string from a file. The file must be opened before reading. Other than text data, Python files may also have binary data. Syntax:

```
file_name.read([count]);
```

The parameter to the function is the number of bytes that you need to read from the file. The method usually begins to read from the beginning of the file. If you don't specify a value for *count*, then the method will read from the file as much as it can. Most probably, the method will read until the file's end. Here is an example:

```
#!/usr/bin/python3

# Opening the file
p = open("friends.txt", "r+")
txt = p.read(10)
print ("The method read the string : ", txt)

# Closing the opened file
p.close()
```

The code returns the following after execution:

```
The method read the string :  nicholas j
```

Note that we had instructed the method to read only 10 bytes from the file, and that is why not all the file contents were read.

File Positions

You may use *tell()* method to tell the current position in a file. This tells where the next read or write will start from the next time you attempt to do so on the file.

If you need to change this position, you can use the *seek(offset[, from])* method. The argument, that is, *offset* specifies the number of bytes that should be moved. The argument *from* specifies the reference position from which bytes should be moved.

If the value of *from* is 0, then the reference position is the starting point of the file. If you set it to 1, then the current position will be used as a reference position. If it is set to 2, the file's end will be used as a reference position.

Example:

```
#!/usr/bin/python3

# Openig the file
p = open("friends.txt", "r+")
str = p.read(10)
print ("The function read the string : ", str)
```

```
# Checking the current position
pos = p.tell()
print ("The current position for the file is : ", pos)

# Reposition the pointer to the beginning
pos = p.seek(0, 0)
str = p.read(10)
print ("The read String again is : ", str)

# Close the opened file
p.close()
```

Run the code from the directory you have stored the file *names.txt*. In my case, it returns the following:

```
The function read the string :  nicholas j
The current position for the file is :   10
The read String again is :  nicholas j
```

You notice that in both cases, the same string was read. We first read the first 10 bytes of the file. This moved the position in the file to 10, as shown in the output. We then called the *seek()* function to reset the position of the file to the beginning. When we issue the read command, it again reads from the beginning. Hence we get the same output.

Renaming Files

The *rename()* method helps in renaming file names, and it takes two arguments. The method takes two arguments, the first one being the current name of the file and the second one being the new name to be given to the file. Note that this method is provided by a Python module named *os*. For you to use the function, you must first import the module. The method takes the following syntax:

```
os.rename(current_filename, new_filename)
```

Example:

```
#!/usr/bin/python3
import os

# Rename the file from friends.txt to colleagues.txt
os.rename( "friends.txt", "colleagues.txt" )
```

We began by importing the *os* module via the *import* keyword. It is after that we have called the *rename()* method. Note the syntax used for calling the method. We began by the module name, that is, os, then the method name, that is, rename(). Two arguments were passed to the method. The first one is the name of the file we need to rename, which is *friendss.txt*. We have then defined the new name we need to give to the file, that is, *colleagues.txt*. That is how files should be renamed in Python.

Deleting Files

The *remove()* method can be used for the deletion of a file. The method is called, and the name of the file to be deleted or removed is passed as the argument. Again, this method is provided in the *os* module. Hence you must first import the module before using the method. The syntax for the method is as follows:

```
os.remove(file_name)
```

Example:

```
#!/usr/bin/python3
import os

# Deleting the file named colleagues.txt
os.remove("colleagues.txt")
```

In the above case, we first imported the *os* module into the script. We have then called the *remove()* method from this module. Again, we used the same syntax to call the method, as we did in our previous example. The name of the file to be deleted is *colleagues.txt*. Hence this has been passed as the argument to the function.

Creating Directories

Files are kept in directories. The os module comes with several methods that can be used for working with directories. The *mkdir()* command provided in the *os* module helps in creating directories in your current directory. The method expects an argument to be passed to it, and this should be the name of the directory to be created. Its syntax involves calling the *os* module first, as shown below:

```
os.mkdir("newdirectoryname")
```

Example:

```
#!/usr/bin/python3
import os

# Create the directory "firstdirectory"
os.mkdir("firstdirectory")
```

In the above example, we have created a directory named *firstdirectory*. The name of the directory has been passed as the argument to the method.

Changing Directory

The *chdir()* method helps in changing the current directory. It takes one argument, which is the name for the directory you need to shift or change to. The syntax for the method is as follows:

```
os.chdir("newdirectoryname")
```

Example:

```
#!/usr/bin/python3
```

```
import os

# Change directory to "/home/seconddirectory"
os.chdir("/home/seconddirectory")
```

In above example, we have simply changed directory to *seconddirectory*.

Current Working Directory

The *getcwd()* method returns the current working directory. The method is defined in os module. Hence it takes the following syntax:

```
os.getcwd()
```

Example:

```
#!/usr/bin/python3
import os

# To return location of current directory
print(os.getcwd())
```

The code will return the current working directory for the user. Notice that the *os.getcwd()* method has been called within the *print()* method. This will help in displaying the current working directory. In my case, it returns the following:

```
C:\Users\admin
```

Deleting Directories

The *rmdir()* method helps in deleting a directory that is passed to it in the form of an argument. Before a directory can be removed, all its contents should first be deleted. Here is the syntax for the method:

```
os.rmdir('dirname')
```

When deleting a directory, a fully qualified name for the directory should be provided. If you don't, the directory will be searched for in the current directory, and it may not be found. Example:

```
#!/usr/bin/python3
import os

# This will delete the "/tmp/firstdirectory" directory.
os.rmdir("/tmp/firstdirectory")
```

Chapter 9- Python Classes and Objects

Python supports the concepts of object-oriented programming. Classes form the backbone of object-oriented programming. A class can be defined as a grouping of data and methods which operate on that data. This means that a class has date and methods, whereby the methods are used for manipulation of the data. The access to the methods of a class is done by use of the dot notation.

To create a Python class, we use the "class" keyword. This keyword is then followed by the name of the class and then a colon(:). Consider the following example:

```
class Class_Name:
```

Consider the Python class given below:

```
class Operations:

    def additionFunction(p,q):
        sum = p + q
        print(sum)

    def subtractionFunction(p,q):
        diff = p - q
        print(diff)

    def multiplicationFunction(p,q):
        prod = p * q
```

```
    print(prod)

  def divisionFunction(p,q):
    div = p / q
    print(div)
```

In the above example, we have created a class named *Operations* with a number of functions. The following syntax can be used to access any of the above methods:

```
Operations.additionFunction(20,30)
```

Here is another example of a Python class:

```
class Citizen:
   'A base class common to all citizens'
   citizen_count = 0

   def __init__(self, name, town):
      self.name = name
      self.town = town
      Citizen.citizen_count += 1

   def displayCount(self):
     print ("Total citizens %d" %
Citizens.citizen_count)

   def showCitizen(self):
      print ("Name : ", self.name,  ", Town: ",
self.town)
```

We began by declaring a variable named "citizen_count", and this is a class variable. This means that the variable will be accessible to all instances which are created from the class.

The "__init__()" is a special method, which is known as the class constructor. It is also referred to as the initialization method, and it will be called whenever a new instance of the class has been called. The other methods for the class are defined in the same manner, with the exception being that the first argument of the method should be "self". Note that this argument will be added to your list by default.

Instantiating Classes

For you to create an instance of a class, you have to use the name of the class to call it and then pass the arguments, which can be accepted by its __init__ method. Consider the example given below:

```
citizen1 = Citizen("John", "Georgia")
```

We can now create the second object of the Citizen class:

```
citizen2 = Citizen("Mercy", "New York")
```

That is how the instances of the class Citizen can be created. We have called the name of the class, and the necessary arguments have been passed to this so as to indicate the real values for them. The first instance is "citizen1", whose name is John and lives in Georgia. The second one is "citizen2" with the name Mercy and lives in New York.

Accessing Attributes

The access to the attributes of an object is done using the dot operator together with the name of the object. The class variables can be used by the use of the class name. This is demonstrated below:

```
citizen1.showCitizen()
citizen2.showCitizen()
print ("The total citizens are %d" %
Citizen.citizen_count)
```

Let us combine all the concepts together to get the following class:

```
class Citizen:
   'A base class common to all citizens'
   citizen_count = 0

   def __init__(self, name, town):
      self.name = name
      self.town = town
      Citizen.citizen_count += 1

   def displayCount(self):
     print ("Total citizens %d" %
Citizens.citizen_count)

   def showCitizen(self):
```

```
        print ("Name : ", self.name,  ", Town: ",
self.town)

#Let us create the first citizen object
citizen1 = Citizen("John", "Georgia")
#Let us create the second object of student
Class"
citizen2 = Citizen("Mercy", "New York")
citizen1.showCitizen()
citizen2.showCitizen()
print ("The total number of citizens is %d" %
Citizen.citizen_count)
```

You can run the program, and you will get the following result:

```
Name :  John , Town:  Georgia
Name :  Mercy , Town:  New York
The total number of citizens is 2
```

Yes, we have our citizens up there, as well as their total count. We have a total of 2 citizens. The variable "citizen_count" was first initialized to 0, and this is being incremented each time a new student is created, or a new object of the "Citizen" class is created.

You should note how the instantiation or the creation of an object from a class is done. See how we have created "citizen1" object from the "Citizen" class:

```
citizen1 = Citizen("John", "Georgia")
```

We have passed the values for the variable name and age inside the class name during the instantiation. The class name has also been used for accessing the value of variables such as the "citizen-count".

You can also remove, modify, or add the attributes of a class and the objects at any time that you need. This is shown below:

```
citizen1.town = 24   # Add an ' town' attribute.
citizen1.name = 'John' # Modify 'name' attribute.
del citizen1.town   # Delete the ' town' attribute.
```

Built-in Attributes for Classes

There are some built-in attributes that are kept by all classes, and to access them, we use the dot operator similar to the other attributes. These include the following:

- __dict__: This is a dictionary with the namespace for the class.
- __doc__: The class documentation string or none, in case it is not defined.
- __name__: The name of the class.
- __module__: The name of the module in which the class has been defined. In the interactive mode, the attribute becomes "__main__".

- __bases__: This is a tuple, possibly empty, having base classes, added in the order that they occur in your base class list.

Consider the example given below:

```python
#!/usr/bin/python3
class Citizen:
   'The base class which is common to all instances'
   citizen_count = 0

   def __init__(self, name, town):
      self.name = name
      self.town = town
      Citizen.citizen_count += 1

   def showCount(self):
     print ("The total number of citizen is %d" % Citizen.citizen_count)

   def showCitizen(self):
       print ("Name : ", self.name,  ", Town: ", self.town)

citizen1 = Citizen("John", "Georgia")
citizen2 = Citizen("Mercy", "New York")
print ("Citizen.__doc__:", Citizen.__doc__)
print ("Citizen.__name__:", Citizen.__name__)
print ("Citizen.__module__:", Citizen.__module__)
print ("Citizen.__bases__:", Citizen.__bases__)
print ("Citizen.__dict__:", Citizen.__dict__ )
```

Run the program, and it will give the following result:

```
Citizen.__doc__: The base class which is common to all instances
Citizen.__name__: Citizen
Citizen.__module__: __main__
Citizen.__bases__: (<class 'object'>,)
Citizen.__dict__: {'citizen_count': 2, '__module__': '__main__', '__init__': <fu
nction Citizen.__init__ at 0x00000000005B7F28>, '__dict__': <attribute '__dict__
' of 'Citizen' objects>, 'showCitizen': <function Citizen.showCitizen at 0x00000
000037C6C80>, '__doc__': 'The base class which is common to all instances', '__w
eakref__': <attribute '__weakref__' of 'Citizen' objects>, 'showCount': <functio
n Citizen.showCount at 0x00000000037C6BF8>}
```

Destroying Objects in Python (Garbage Collection)

In Python, any unneeded objects are deleted automatically so that we can free up the memory space. The process of reclaiming the blocks of memory which are not used in Python is referred to as Garbage Collection. The collector for garbage collection in Python usually runs during the execution of a program. It will be triggered the reference to the count has reached zero (0). The value for this usually changes as the aliases which point to a particular object change.

The reference count for an object will increase after a new name is assigned to it or after it has been placed in a new container such a dictionary, a list or a tuple. Once the del statement is used to delete the object, the value of count will decrease, or once its reference has gone out of scope or once the reference is reassigned.

After the reference count of an object has reached 0 in Python, it will be collected automatically. Consider the example given below:

```
p = 30        # Create an object <30>
q = p         # Increase the ref. count for <30>
z = [q]       # Increase the ref. count for <30>

del p         # Decrease the ref. count for <30>
q = 90        # Decrease the ref. count for <30>
z[0] = -1     # Decrease the ref. count for <30>
```

However, you may expect to know when Python has done garbage collection on a particular instance. This is not possible. However, in Python, it is possible for a class to implement a destructor named "__del__()" which will be invoked when a particular object is almost destroyed. Any non-memory resources which are not being used by an instance can be cleaned by the use of this method.

When the "__del__()" destructor is used, it will print the name of the class of the instance which is being destroyed. Consider the example given below:

```
#!/usr/bin/python3

class Center:
    def __init( self, p=0, q=0):
        self.p = p
        self.q = q
    def __del__(self):
```

```
        class_name = self.__class__.__name__
        print (class_name, "destroyed")

ct1 = Center()
ct2 = ct1
ct3 = ct1
print (id(ct1), id(ct2), id(ct3)) # to print the object ids
del ct1
del ct2
del ct3
```

Run the above program and you will observe the result shown below:

```
55119488 55119488 55119488
Center destroyed
```

The best idea for you is to create your classes in some separate files. You can then use the "import" statement so as to import these classes into your main program. Suppose the code given above was created in "center.py" and it has no executable code, then we can do this as follows:

```
#!/usr/bin/python3
import center
ct1=center.Center()
```

Method Overriding in Python

It is possible for you to override the methods of the parent class. This is because you may be in need of getting a different functionality from this function. Consider the example given below:

```
#!/usr/bin/python3

# defining the parent class
class ParentClass:
    def method1(self):
        print ('Parent method called')

# defining the child class
class ChildClass(ParentClass):
    def method1(self):
        print ('Child method called')

# instance of the child class
c = ChildClass()

# The child calls an overridden method
c.method1()
```

In the above example, we have created a method named "method1()" in the parent class. This method has been defined again in the child class, and it is calling a different print function as specified in the child class. The program will give the following result once executed:

```
Child method called
```

In the first definition of the method parent class, the method was to print "Parent method called". However, we need it to print something different from this, as shown in the above output. That is why we had to override this method!

Data Hiding

In Python, the attributes which have been defined in a class can be made visible or not visible outside that class. If you need to disable the direct visibility of attributes from a class, you should write their names with a double underscore (__) as a prefix. Consider the following example:

```
#!/usr/bin/python3

class CounterExample:
    __x = 0

    def count(self):
        self.__x += 1
        print (self.__x)

y = CounterExample()
y.count()
y.count()
print (y.__x)
```

Run the above program and observe the output that you get. This should be as follows:

```
Traceback (most recent call last):
  File "C:\Users\admin\lsvsts.py", line 13, in <module>
    print (y.__x)
AttributeError: 'CounterExample' object has no attribute '__x'
```

The output from the program is an error. This is because we are trying to access an attribute that is not accessible. What happens after you have used a double underscore to define an attribute is that the Python internally changes it to include the name of the class, and this makes the attribute protected. If you need to successes in accessing such an attribute, you must use the following syntax:

```
object._className__attributeName
```

The following is a modified version of the above program which shows how you can access the above attribute:

```
#!/usr/bin/python3

class CounterExample:
    __x = 0

    def count(self):
        self.__x += 1
        print (self.__x)

y = CounterExample()
y.count()
```

```
y.count()

print (y._CounterExample__x)
```

This will give the following result after execution:

```
1
2
2
```

This shows that our attribute has been accessed successively despite it having been made invisible.

Inheritance

In Python, you don't have to create your class from scratch but you can inherit from ma certain class, normally known as the "parent" class. The parent class should be place in parenthesis after the definition of the new class.

Since the parent class has some attributes, the new class, which is the child class will be allowed to use these attributes in such a manner that they have been defined in the child class. It is also possible for the child class to override the methods and the data members from the parent class.

Class inheritance in Python takes the following syntax:

```
class ChildClassName (ParentClass1[,
ParentClass2, ...]):
```

Note that in the above syntax, the child class is inheriting from multiple parent classes as Python supports this. Consider the example given below:

```
#!/usr/bin/python3

# define parent class
class ParentClass:
   parentValue = 78
   def __init__(self):
      print ("Parent constructor called")

   def parentMethod(self):
      print ('Parent method called')

   def setValue(self, value):
      ParentClass.parentValue = value

   def getValue(self):
      print ("The parent value is :", ParentClass.parentValue)

# defining the child class class
ChildClass(ParentClass):
   def __init__(self):
      print ("Child constructor called")

   def childMethod(self):
      print ('Child method called')

cc = ChildClass()        # instance of child
```

```
cc.childMethod()      # child calls its method
cc.parentMethod()  # calls parent's method
cc.setValue(89)    # again call parent's method
cc.getValue()      # again call parent's method
```

Run the program and observe the output it gives. This should be as shown below:

```
Child constructor called
Child method called
Parent method called
The parent value is : 89
```

In this example, we have the parent class named "ParentClass". We have defined an attribute named "parentValue" in this class whose value has been initialized to 78. We have also defined a method named "parentMethod()" in the parent class. The method for setting the value of the attribute, that is, "setValue()" and the method for getting the value of the attribute "getValue()" have also been defined within this class.

We have then defined a child class named "ChildClass" which is inheriting the properties of the ParentClass. This means that the class "ChildClass" will have access to all the attributes and methods which have been defined in the class "ParentClass". In the child class, we have created a method named "childMethod()". In the line "cc = ChildClass()", we have created an instance of the child class and this has been named "cc". This instance has then been used for accessing the attributes and methods of the parent class, which is the

"ParentClass". The initial value of the parentValue was 78. However, in the child class, we have called the setValue() method to reset this value to 89. This explains the source of the above output!

The derivation of a class from multiple classes can be done as shown below:

```
class X:          # define a class named X
.....

class Y:          # define a class named Y
.....

class Z(X, Y):    # The class Z should inherit
from class X and Y
.....
```

Note that the classes from which the child class should inherit are separated by the use of a comma. That is the good thing with Python in that you can inherit from multiple classes at once!

If you need to know the relationship between two classes in Python, you can use either the "isinstance()" or the "issubclass()" methods. These two take the following syntax:

- issubclass(sub, sup)- this function will return true if "sub" is a subclass of "sup", the superclass.
- isinstance(obj, Class)- this will return a true if the "obj" is an instance of the class "Class".

Operator Overloading

Suppose you have two-dimensional vectors that you have defined, and you need to add them. In most cases, the Python interpreter will warn at you.

However, once you have defined the "__add__" method, it will be possible for you to perform the vector addition, and the + operator will be working as you expect. Consider the example given below:

```
#!/usr/bin/python3
class AddVectors:
    def __init__(self, p, q):
        self.p = p
        self.q = q

    def __str__(self):
        return 'Vector (%d, %d)' % (self.p, self.q)

    def __add__(self,r):
```

```
        return AddVectors(self.p + r.p, self.q +
r.q)

vector1 = AddVectors(7,3)
vector2 = AddVectors(-4,17)
print (vector1 + vector2)
```

After the execution of the above program, you will get the result shown below:

```
          Vector (3, 20)
```

In the above example, operator overloading has been implemented in the *"line return AddVectors(self.p + r.p, self.q + r.q)."* This is because we have specified another use of the + operator unlike what it is normally used for.

Conclusion

This marks the end of this guide. Python is an object-oriented programming language that can be used for a wide variety of tasks. Python is a simple programming language, characterized by its easy syntax and semantics. This has made it the best programming language to any person who is a complete beginner to computer programming. In developed countries, Python is taught to kids due to its simplicity. Python is an interpreted language, meaning that the Python interpreter works on your code line-by-line. To get started with Python programming, you need to have a text editor and the Python interpreter installed. It is after this that you can choose the model that you need to follow in writing and running your codes.

In the interactive mode of programming, you open the Python's interactive terminal and directly invoke the Python interpreter. In the script mode programming, you write your scripts in a text editor, save the script in a file with a *.py* extension then you invoke the Python interpreter on the file. The *.py* extension marks the file as a Python file. Python supports many features that we can use when writing programs and developing applications. The popularity of Python is also rising steadily because of its compatibility with many machine learning libraries. Examples of such libraries include TensorFlow, PyTorch, Keras, Scikit-Learn etc.

www.ingramcontent.com/pod-product-compliance
Lightning Source LLC
Chambersburg PA
CBHW071415210526
45465CB00001B/395